Ismar J. Peritz

Woman in the Ancient Hebrew Cult

Ismar J. Peritz

Woman in the Ancient Hebrew Cult

ISBN/EAN: 9783337315993

Printed in Europe, USA, Canada, Australia, Japan

Cover: Foto ©Lupo / pixelio.de

More available books at **www.hansebooks.com**

WOMAN IN THE ANCIENT HEBREW CULT.

BY

ISMAR J. PERITZ, A.M., PH.D. (HARV.),

PROFESSOR OF SEMITIC LANGUAGES AND ARCHÆOLOGY, SYRACUSE UNIVERSITY.

Reprinted from JOURNAL OF BIBLICAL LITERATURE (1898, Part II.), published by the Society of Biblical Literature and Exegesis.

6 1⁄2

PREFATORY NOTE

THIS dissertation is substantially the thesis presented to the Faculty of Arts and Sciences of Harvard University for the degree of Doctor of Philosophy in the Department of Semitic Languages and History.

The subject itself was suggested to me by the discussion in the movement to secure for women admission to the highest legislative council, the General Conference, of the Methodist Episcopal Church. In this discussion the so-called Biblical argument, taken as pointing to woman's inferior position in the cult, played an important part. There is, however, no attempt in these pages to deal with that question in its ecclesiastical relation; and I can lay claim to a contribution in that direction only in so far as a correct view of woman's relation to the ancient Hebrew cult affects her position in religious affairs in general.

To Professors C. H. Toy, LL.D., and D. G. Lyon, Ph.D., of Harvard University, my teachers in the Semitic branches for the period of three years, I express herewith my indebtedness, not only for many suggestions, but chiefly for the method and point of view underlying my investigation.

I. J. P.

SYRACUSE, N.Y., December, 1898.

CONTENTS.

Woman in the Ancient Hebrew Cult.

PROF. ISMAR J. PERITZ.

SYRACUSE, N.Y.

1. Introduction. Current View of Woman's Relation to the Cult.

THE opinion has found considerable currency that woman, on account of her sex, was disqualified to perform the duties of the religious cult among the Hebrews; that in the absence of males in the family, the cult of the deceased could not be perpetuated. The chief representatives of this view are Stade, Schwally, Benzinger, and Nowack. Benzinger (*Hebräische Archäologie*, p. 140) has given it amplest expression; and, in order to have it clearly before us, I quote his words in full: "Noch an einem anderen Punkt zeigt sich die Inferiorität der Frau deutlich: die Frau war nicht fähig zur Ausübung des Kultus. Die Sitte der Schwagerehe setzt die Anschauung voraus, dass Frau und Töchter nicht im Stande sind, den Kultus des Toten zu pflegen. Aus demselben Grund kam ihnen nur ein sehr beschränktes Erbrecht zu, ebensowenig wurden der Frau nach dem Tod kultische Ehren zu teil. Nur als Ehefrau war ihr eine gewisse Teilnahme am Kulte des Mannes gestattet. Bis auf den heutigen Tag hat sich bei den Juden diese Vorstellung erhalten: die Frauen dürfen dem Gottesdienst in der Synagoge anwohnen, die Mädchen sind davon ausgeschlossen. Nicht minder wird im Islâm die Frau als unfähig zur Kultusübung betrachtet. Dass schon frühe einzelne Frauen als Prophetinnen auftreten, ist eine Ausnahme, welche die Regel bestätigt."

Nowack (*Hebräische Archäologie* i. 344 f., 348) is less sweeping in his statements, but also affirms that the levirate law had for its main object to provide male descent for the dead, because woman was unqualified to participate in the cult; that this disqualification also lay at the basis of the Hebrew laws of inheritance; and that only the son, or the nearest male, and not the female, was qualified to transmit the cult of the testator.

The expression of this view reaches, it seems to me, the strangest height, when Schwally (*ZATW.* xi. 176 ff.) endeavors to explain the word זָכָר, 'male,' as connected with הִזְכִּיר בְּשֵׁם אלהים, 'to call in cult upon God,' and meaning therefore first 'a cultic person,' then, on the assumption, according to the view in question, that this cultic person can be in all Israelitish and Semitic antiquity only a man, meaning, secondly, 'a male.' This sexual meaning was then, thirdly, transferred from men to animals, and reached the highest point of development in the Arabic and Aramaic in the meaning, fourthly, "das männliche Glied." Leaving out of consideration the assumption as to cult, such a view of an etymological development from a distinct spiritual meaning to the lowest physical will never commend itself as an improvement on the older view represented by Gesenius, *s.v.*

None of the three authorities mentioned seems to speak from independent investigation of the subject of woman's relation to the Hebrew or Semitic cult. All three are evidently dependent upon Stade, and simply follow him.

Stade reaches his conclusion in a peculiar manner. He is dealing with the Hebrew family in pre-prophetic time, and he finds in the customs of mourning evidences of a cult of the dead and indications of ancestor-worship. He concludes from these indications that ancestor-worship was a prime factor in the formation of the ancient Israelitish family. Here he begins to call attention to similarities in the organization of the ancient Greek, Roman, and Indian families, and to draw parallels between them and the Semitic. The ancient Indo-Germanic family was a "Cultgenossenschaft," held together by the common bond of worship of the ancestors of the family, whose altar is the family altar, and whose priest is the father and the lord of the house. This cult explains the most ancient laws of the people. Can similar ancient Hebrew laws find a similar explanation? In answering this question affirmatively Stade proceeds to instance the law of inheritance. This law among the ancient Hebrews, as among the ancient Greeks and Romans, was originally that of agnates. In ancient Israel the son only is the heir, not the daughter. Stade asserts that wherever this law of inheritance is found, the ground for it is that only the son, or the nearest male relative, taking his place as the heir, can perpetuate the cult of the testator (*Geschichte* i. 388–391).

It is important to observe that Stade's conclusion, denying woman her share in the ancient Hebrew cult, is not based upon any direct evidence derived from the Old Testament itself, but upon a remote and supposed analogy which connects a question of cult with that of the law of inheritance, and upon an utter disregard of all phenomena in the Old Testament that may point the other way.

The connection of the law of inheritance with the admission to the cult, and the explanation of the former from this source, are entirely forced and unsatisfactory. That the inheritance in old Israel was restricted to agnates is true enough (Nowack, *Arch.* i. 348 f.); but we may well ask whether there is not a simpler explanation of the fact. The weakness of Stade's position becomes very apparent when, in his attempt to support his view of the dependence of the right to inherit upon admission to the cult, he refers to Gen. $15^{2f.}$ as the solitary evidence. Now, the ancient custom that in default of a son the slave of the master becomes heir may prove that Abraham had no son, but how it can prove that Eliezer was the last representative of the family cult, save on the assumption of that which Stade endeavors to prove, I cannot see.

But the fact of woman's exclusion from the Hebrew laws of inheritance does not need explanation from her relation to the cult. There is a better way. W. Robertson Smith mentions a similar law among the Arabs. Smith shows that antique Arab society had its basis not in the patriarchal authority, the family, but in the stock or kinship tribe, an organization that has for its object offence and defence, and that the whole law of the old Arabs resolves itself into a law of war, in which blood-feud, blood-wite, and booty are the points on which everything turns. The law of inheritance there follows the law of booty. The tribe owned the property of which the individual had only a usufruct, and which fell to be divided after his death like the spoils of war. The right of inheritance belonged to the active members of the tribe. This explains the relation of woman to the law of inheritance, and is in accordance with the old law of Medina, quoted by Smith, in which women were excluded from inheritance on the principle that "none can be heirs who do not take part in battle, drive booty, and protect property." See W. R. Smith, *Kinship and Marriage*, pp. 33–58, and his note on "Law of Inheritance," p. 263.

Now, it is a well-recognized fact that the affinity in social organization and ancient law is far greater between the Arabs and the Hebrews than between the Semites and the Greeks and Romans. And so woman's exclusion from inheritance finds here, it seems to me, a natural, reasonable, and more direct explanation, and does not need the assumption that woman was excluded from the ancient Hebrew cult. It thus appears that the current opinion on woman's relation to the Hebrew cult is by no means based upon a special and direct investigation of the subject. This phase of Hebrew antiquity has so far received no critical treatment.[1] Because in later Levitical legislation man is made prominent in the cult, and later Judaism has in Herod's Temple a "Court of Women," and the Mishna exempts woman from reading the Shema' and the ritual of the phylacteries (*Berakoth* 3[3]), and in the Middle Ages woman was relegated to the galleries of the synagogues,[2] and Jewish men now pray: "Blessed art thou, Lord, our God, King of the world, that thou hast not made me a woman" (*Hebrew Prayer Book:* part of the daily morning prayer), and because Islam excludes woman from the cult, it has been taken for granted that this exclusion was from the beginning a distinctive feature of Semitic cult. The facts on the subject, as contained in the Old Testament, and supplied by other Semitic religions, have not been collected and squarely looked in the face. To supply this evident lack is the object of this essay. My method of treatment is to collect, arrange, and explain some of the more prominent facts in regard to woman's position in other Semitic cults in general, but more especially, *all* the facts bearing upon woman's position in the ancient and later Hebrew cult as contained in the Old Testament. The conclusion to which the facts thus treated have led me, if I may here anticipate, is that the Semites in general, and the Hebrews in particular, and the latter especially in the earlier periods of their history, exhibit no tendency to discriminate between man and woman so far as regards participation in religious practices, but that woman participates in all the essentials of the cult, both as worshipper and official; and that only in later time, with the progress in the development of the cult itself, a tendency appears, not so much, however, to exclude woman from the cult, as rather to make man prominent in it.[3]

[1] Schechter, in his *Studies in Judaism*, under the caption, "Woman in Temple and Synagogue," touches lightly, and in a popular way, upon some of the surface facts of the subject. His essay cannot be regarded as a critical contribution to the subject, and in fact he does not lay claim to such a contribution. See p. 313.

[2] Cf. Israel Abrahams, *Jewish Life in the Middle Ages*, p. 25 f.

[3] I hope, at some future time, as a second part of the subject, to treat fully of the causes of woman's later inferior position in the cult, and her final, apparently entire, exclusion from it.

2. Woman in Other Semitic Cults.

That we have reason to look to other Semitic cults for light has been fully demonstrated by the researches of W. R. Smith, embodied in his *Religion of the Semites*. The fundamental institutions of the Israelites had a common origin with those of the other Semitic peoples. The relation of woman to the other Semitic cults has therefore a vital bearing on our question, and must all the more receive some attention, since Schwally (*ZATW*. xi. 178) claims that "im israelitischen, überhaupt im ganzen semitischen Altertum," man only possessed the qualification to perform independently the duties of the religious cult.

1. *Woman in the Arabic Cult.*

Islam is no such ancient nor unadulterated source as to supply much that is helpful in the investigation of the early Hebrew cult. It is far different with pre-Islamic, Arabic heathenism. Here we may well go with confidence for analogies and explanations. We are not, therefore, like Benzinger, so much concerned with the relation of woman to the cult of Islam as with her relation to the cult of Arabic heathenism. Fortunately, meagre as the source in general is, it yields material enough to leave beyond any question woman's relation to Arabic cult. The facts, as collected mainly from Wellhausen's *Reste arabischen Heidentumes*, lead to the conclusion that this relation is one of almost perfect parity with that of man, there being not the slightest indication that the question of sex from a religious point of view ever comes into consideration.

(1) *Female Divinities.* — Female divinities are numerous, and play a very important rôle in Arabic heathenism. The Jinns even were mostly feminine (Wellh., *Heid.*, p. 135). Local divinities of Mecca were Isâf and Nâila, man and wife (p. 73). In the Ka'ba at Mecca stood a dove of aloe wood, a fact pointing to the great Semitic goddess (p. 70). Suvâ', one of the five "idols of the people of Noah," was worshipped by the Beni Hamdân, and in the form of a woman; so a late tradition says, which, however, according to Wellhausen, is not reliable (p. 16). According to Epiphanius the worship of Dhu lShara was associated with that of his virgin mother (p. 46). Shams was a goddess (p. 56). But chief of all are "the three daughters of Allah," the goddesses Al Lât, Manât, and Al 'Uzza, whose worship possessed more vitality and importance than that of all the male divinities, Allah only excepted. All Arabia was most zealously

devoted to them, the polemic against them in the Koran being but a small part of the evidence of this fact (p. 21 ff., p. 71). A religion that pays such homage to female divinities is not likely to discriminate against woman in matters of cult; at any rate only the most positive testimony can carry any weight in the matter.

(2) *Women as Devotees.* — Women frequented the places of worship. At the annual Ḥajj at Mecca married and unmarried women were present (p. 85). The reference in Yaqut to the backs of the women jostling at Dhu lKhalaṣa is an indication in what throngs the women attended the sanctuaries (Wellh., p. 43; Smith, *Kinship*, p. 295).

But the women's devotion was not confined to simple attendance; they brought their votive offerings. There is ancient testimony to the fact that the women worshipped Al 'Uzza "daily with sacrifices and gifts" (Wellh., p. 37; cf. also pp. 112, 101).

The two principal acts of Arabic worship, the 'stroking' (*tamassuḥ*), and (most important of all) the *ṭawāf*, or act of encircling the sacred stone, were participated in by the women as well as by the men (Wellh., pp. 52, 105 f., 118).

In the cult of the dead the women had even more than their share. It was theirs to chant the rhythmical dirge; the institution of the professional mourning men is later than that of the mourning women (p. 160).[4] The regulation that woman during the period of her purification must not approach the sanctuary (pp. 52 and 118) is but the evidence of the single exception that proves her inclusion in the cult. For an interesting story of the conversion of a Dausite and his wife, illustrating many points of the intimate association of man with woman in religion, see Wellh., *Heid.*, p. 45.

(3) *Woman as Cultic Official.* — Arabic heathenism had two chief cultic officials: *sâdin* (temple watchman), or *ḥâjib* (doorkeeper), the temple servant or priest, and *kâhin*, seer, prophet. In the latter class women are numerous (Wellh., p. 130); but of the woman *sâdin* there is not a single instance that I can find. But this fact finds a simple explanation as soon as the nature of the office is examined. The *sâdin* was not a priest whose specific prerogative it was to officiate at the altar. Such an official the Arabs never had. He was not needed for sacrificing, and, though the sacred lot was in his keeping, and he, in general, officiated at the casting of the sacred

[4] Circumcision was practised, among some tribes, upon girls (p. 154 f., 168). But this custom, found also among certain uncivilized tribes in Africa, was merely one feature in the consecration of all the members of the tribe to the deity.

lots, even that could be done without him (Wellh., p. 129). The *sâdin* or *ḥâjib*, as the names indicate, was the watchman, the door-keeper of the sanctuary. Arabic nomadic life had given a peculiar form of duty to this office. In general the sanctuaries did not wander with the tribes, but remained stationary; but there are cases where the idol did share in the nomadic life, and was carried into battle like the ark of Jahveh (Wellh., pp. 18 and 129). Cases of theft of idols, even, are not unheard of (p. 18). The *sâdin* became in this manner the resident, the defender, and, in time, the actual possessor of the sanctuary. By a natural law of selection, the office of watcher, protector, and possessor would fall to man and not to woman. The absence of woman from this office cannot therefore be taken as implying a discrimination against woman in reference to the cult.

This view is confirmed by the fact that woman was not excluded from the office of *kâhin*, which carried with it far greater cultic significance. This significance becomes all the more apparent when the original position of the *kâhin* is recognized. There is every reason for accepting the conclusion of W. R. Smith, Wellhausen, and most moderns, that the office of the *sâdin* was originally included in that of the *kâhin*, which corresponded very nearly to that of the early Hebrew *kôhen*. In course of development the *kâhins* branched off from the general priestly body, carrying with them the principal part of its duty and the ancient title of honor, and leaving behind them a class of officials who sank into mere *æditui* (Wellh., p. 134; W. R. Smith, *Journal of Philology* xiii. 278). The *kâhin* therefore was originally the great official of the cult, and women, as stated, are frequently found holding this office.

It thus appears that the testimony of Arabic heathenism on woman's relation to the cult is comprehensive, clear, and uniform. Whether as divinity, devotee, or cultic official, woman shares cultic duties with man, and in matters of religion there is no sign of any discrimination against her on account of her sex.

2. *Woman in Assyro-Babylonian, Phœnician, and other Semitic Cults.*

Babylonian and Assyrian cults do not furnish altogether as safe a basis for comparison with the Hebrew cult as that of Arabic heathenism. Babylonian and Assyrian religions, as is generally held, are syncretistic, mixed with non-Semitic elements, and developed under physical and moral conditions different from those which determined the Hebrew development. This is in great measure true also of the Phœnician cult — a result due, no doubt, to its close relation to the Assyro-Babylonian. One feels the need, therefore, of caution in the use of material from these sources. Yet there are certain general features which recur with striking uniformity in all parts of the Semitic field, as W. R. Smith has said (*Rel. of Sem.*, p. 14 ff.). The relation of woman to the cult, it may be safely asserted, is one of these. As my purpose is simply to allow a side light from this direction to fall upon the main question, it will not require an exhaustive treatment.

(1) *Female Divinities.* — It will not be necessary to name all of the numerous female divinities of the Assyro-Babylonian pantheon. As the representative of them all, we may call to mind the Babylonian Ishtar, who was venerated as the mother goddess, the queen, head and firstborn of all gods. (Cf. W. R. Smith, *Rel.*, p. 56 ff.) Among the other female divinities may be named Damkina, Nana, Nin-gal, Gula, Anunit, and Zarpanit. In pairs often occur the divinities: as, Bel and Belit; Ea and Damkina.

The Phœnicians have by the side of בעל a בעלת, both distinguished by many additional names, expressing either attributes or names of cities devoted to their worship. Besides, they worshipped עשתרת, Astarte, the great Semitic goddess, and תנת, Tanith. Cf. Baethgen, *Beiträge*, pp. 29, 31, 26 ff.; Baudissin, *PRE*[3]. *s.v.* Astarte, Baal; Pietschmann, *Geschichte d. Phoenizier*, p. 182 ff.

The Moabites worshipped by the side of כמש an עשתר כמש who was most probably a female divinity. (Cf. Baudissin, *PRE*[3]. ii. 150, 156, and Baethgen, pp. 14, 256.) To her Mesha, according to his inscription, devoted the Israelitish captives. Cf. the inscription of King Mesha on the Moabite stone, l. 17.

The Aramæans worshipped by the side of Hadad the female divinity Atargatis, who was the great Syrian goddess, even outranking Hadad. Cf. Baethgen, 68, 74.

(2) *Women as Devotees.* — It would be safe to let this question rest on *a priori* grounds: that cults which pay such homage to female divinities cannot discriminate in matters of cult against the female sex. But there is all the direct testimony that is needed. Woman's intimate relation to the divinity finds expression in some of the female names, viz. אמתמלקרת and מתמלקרת, "Handmaid of Melkart"; חתמלקרת, "Sister of Melkart"; חנמלקרת, "Grace of Melkart"; cf. Euting, *Sammlung Karthag. Inschriften*, 153, 320, 213, 165, quoted by Baethgen, p. 21; so also אמתעשתרת (*CIS.* 46), חתמלכת (*CIS.* 231), נעמלכת (*CIS.* 41).

But the most abundant evidence we find in the Old Testament itself in the numerous allusions to woman's participation in foreign cults, of which I treat further on. See p. 120.

(3) *Woman as Cultic Official.* — Meissner, in his *Beiträge zum altbabylonischen Privatrecht* (pp. 8 and 111, § 12), speaks of financial functions of priests and priestesses, the latter's official position in the temple being indicated by *SAL* (or *UD*) *Šamaš*; cf. also Peiser, *Babylonische Verträge d. Berl. Mus.*, pp. xvii–xxix.

There were priestesses of Ishtar at Uruk (cf. Jeremias, *Izdubar-Nimrod*, p. 59 f.).

Prophetesses, who tell the messages of the gods, are mentioned in connection with the 'seers' in the text of Gudea. Cf. Amiaud, "The Inscription of Telloh," *Records of the Past*, New Series, i. 42, ii. 78.

To the same class of officials belong, most probably, also the priestesses or prophetesses whose names are attached to the oracular responses of Istar of Arbela. Cf. Pinches, "The Oracle of Istar of Arbela," *Records of the Past*, New Series, v. 129 ff.; Tiele, *Gesch. d. Rel.*, p. 195.

These scattered references have led me to go carefully through Delitzsch's *Assyrisches Handwörterbuch* in quest of designations of these female officials. To give this subject the thorough treatment it needs would require too long a digression, and I therefore present these designations in a simple alphabetical order: —

(1) *uḫâtu*, eine weibliche Hierodule, näher Dienerin der Göttin Istar von Erech. They appear also as "Klagefrauen beim Tammuz-Fest" (Del., p. 41).
(2) *êpištu*, fem. of part. *êpišu*, Hexe (p. 119).
(3) *âšiptu*, fem. of *âšipu*, Beschwörer (p. 247).
(4) *zirmaštu*, ein Epitheton, bez. Name der Zauberin oder Hexe (p. 264).
(5) *ḫarimtu* auch *ḫarmatu*, eine weibliche Hierodule, näher Dienerin der Göttin Istar zu Erech (p. 290).
(6) *kaššaptu*, fem. of *kaššapu*, Zauberin, Hexe (p. 360).
(7) *maḫḫutu*, fem. of *maḫḫu*, der von Ekstase befallene, von Sinnen seiende (vgl. מְשֻׁגָּע), Prophet, Wahrsager, *μάντις*, bez. Prophetin (p. 397).
(8) *ḳadištu* (*gadištu*), Hierodule, eine dem Dienste der Göttin Istar geweihte und dadurch entweihte Jungfrau (vgl. קְדֵשָׁה). The term is also used of the Zauberin und Hexe (p. 581).
(9) *šabrâtu*, fem. of *šabrû*, eine best. Berufsart, viell. Magier, Seher (p. 639).

On woman's position as official in Phœnician cult, the Eshmunazar inscription furnishes a word that is of the highest import. The Sidonian king, naming his mother, calls her not only אמעשתרת, but he designates her also כהנת עשתרת, the feminine form of כהן, found here for the first time. Cf. *CIS.* 3, l. 14 f.

3. *Old Testament References to Woman's Relation to other Semitic Cults.*

As furnishing us with a view of the relation of woman to other and especially Semitic cults, the allusions in the Old Testament must not be overlooked. These allusions cover two points: (1) The worship of strange gods by devotees who were either Canaanites or immigrants on Israelitish soil, and (2) the worship of strange gods by the Hebrew women themselves. The chief means by which the first could establish itself alongside of the Hebrew cult was intermarriage. As Professor Moore says: "The connubium in itself involved the recognition of one another's religion, and was naturally followed by participation in the cultus" (*Judges*, p. 83). Hence, the result of such unions is uniformly stated to have been the establishment of the foreign cult (cf. Ju. $3^{5 f.}$ 1 Ki. 11^{1-8}). But our chief interest here lies in the intense zeal which the strange wives of the Hebrews manifested in the observance and propagation of their native cults. Here, of course, Jezebel will first come to mind.[5] But that she was by no means the only instance can be easily gathered from such notices as that which speaks of Solomon's readiness to provide the means for the worship of his "strange wives which burnt incense and sacrificed unto their gods" (1 Ki. 11^{8}), and more still from the numerous Deuteronomic passages which ascribe the spread of idolatry to these intermarriages, and strictly forbid them on that ground (Ex. $34^{15 f.}$ Dt. $7^{3 f.}$ Jos. $23^{12 f.}$). It will be seen that these facts gathered from the Old Testament confirm the view arrived at from the more direct sources, that woman's part in the other Semitic cults was intensely active.

But this activity was not confined to non-Hebrew women. Even before Jezebel, Maacah, the mother of Asa (1 Ki. 15^{13}), had manifested her zeal for the Canaanitish cult of Astarte (cf. Stade, *Gesch.* i. 355; Baethgen, *Beiträge*, p. 218; Baudissin, *PRE*[3]. *s.v.* Astarte, Aschera) by erecting to her worship a מפלצת, which was probably nothing else than an אשרה, which Asa in the progress of a religious reformation hews down, and burns in the valley of the Kidron, and at the same time punishes his mother's idolatrous tendencies by depriving her of the rank of the queen-mother. As the Jezebel of the southern kingdom appears Athaliah, probably Jezebel's daughter (cf. Stade, *Gesch.* i. 524, note 2). That her zealous endeavor to establish the Phœnician cult on Judæan soil was not void of suc-

[5] Cf. 1 Ki. $16^{31 ff.}$ $18^{4. 13. 19}$ 19^{2} 2 Ki. 3^{18} 9^{22b}.

cess is evident from the bitterness with which she is mentioned (cf. 2 Ki. $8^{18.26f.}$ 2 Chr. 21^{6} $22^{2f.}$ 24^{7}).

In the time of the prophet Jeremiah (7^{18} $44^{15ff.}$) the Hebrew women vied with one another in their devotion to the Assyrian cult of Ishtar, whom they worshipped under the name of מלכת השמים (cf. Baudissin, *PRE*[3]. *s.v.* Astarte), claiming it to be a well-established cult, the practice of which had always been a source of prosperity, and its neglect the cause of adversity ($44^{17f.}$). One feature of the cult is characteristically feminine: while the children gather wood, and the fathers kindle the fire, the women knead the dough, and bake the cakes in the moon-shaped form to portray the goddess (cf. v. Orelli, *Jeremia*, on 44^{19}; Wellhausen, *Heid.*, p. 38 f.).

To this cult most probably belongs the reference 2 Ki. 23^{7b}, where the Massoretic בתים might well be corrected (on the basis of Cod. Alex. χεττιειμ = כתיים probably for כתנים) to כְּתֻנּוֹת, χιτῶν (Lucian στολάς), *tunica* (cf. Klostermann *in loc.*), pointing to an activity on the part of some of the women (perhaps the קדשות) in providing garments probably used in the act of the worship of Astarte; for the custom of changing garments in preparation for the approach of the divinity, and of priests supplying such garments, finds illustration in other cults (cf. Wellh., *Heid.*, pp. 52, 106; Gen. 35^{2} 2 Ki. 10^{22}). This explanation of the passage, it seems to me, will furnish the best answer to Stade's rather too ready expedient that the second half of the verse is a "naïve Glosse eines Späteren" (*Gesch.* i. 653, note 4).

To Ezekiel (8^{14}) we are indebted for the bare mention of the Hebrew women's devotion to the worship of Tammuz.[6] The phraseology with which he describes the worship, "there sat the women weeping for Tammuz," leaves its identity with that of Adonis under his Babylonian name, the characteristic of which was lamentation, without a doubt (cf. Baudissin, *Studien* i. 35, 300 ff.).

Woman's part as devotee in the worship of Melek, the sacrificing of children in the Valley of Hinnom, which dates back as far as Ahaz, and reached frightful dimensions in the dark days of the seventh century,[7] is not directly stated in the Old Testament. Professor Moore, in his article, "The Image of Moloch" (in this JOURNAL, xvi. 163), cites a passage from Plutarch (*De Superstitione*, c. 13),

[6] That Zechariah's "mourning for Hadadrimmon" (Zech. 12^{11}) has no connection with Tammuz or Adonis worship has been shown by Baudissin (*Studien* i. 295 ff.).

[7] Cf. W. R. Smith, *Encycl. Brit*[9]. xvi. 696; Stade, *Gesch.* i. 609 f.; Driver, *Deut.*, p. 222 f.

according to which the Carthaginians used to sacrifice their own children, and those who had no offspring of their own used to buy children from the poor, and slaughter them, as if they were lambs or birds. At these sacrifices the mother stood by, unmoved, without a groan. That there was also no distinction of sex in that cult as far as the victim itself was concerned is evident from the recurring phrase "to make one's son or daughter to pass through the fire to Moloch" (2 Ki. 23^{10} Jer. 32^{35}, *etc.*). There is sufficient reason to suppose, then, that the general terms "children of Judah" (Jer. 7^{30}), "inhabitants of Jerusalem" (19^{3}), "this city" (19^{8}), used by the prophets condemning the practice include both men and women. (Cf. Jer. 32^{32} Ez. $16^{2\,ff.}$, and compare Jer. 19^{13} with 44^{15}.)[8]

It appears then that the facts thus collected from the Old Testament on woman's relation to the foreign cults give very clear testimony, and that it is throughout to the effect that woman, whether native or Hebrew, shared in all the religious activities, and often excelled in manifesting religious zeal. Well might the Deuteronomic lawgiver, aware of woman's religious interest and zeal, provide the most drastic measures for its destruction (cf. Dt. $13^{7-12\,(6-11)}$ 17^{2-5}).

3. Woman as Devotee in the Jahveh Cult.

1. *The Presence of Women at the Sanctuary and Religious Gatherings.*

Hannah and Peninnah, as also the daughters of Elkanah, were accustomed to go up to the yearly religious gathering before Jahveh in Shiloh (1 S. $1^{1\,ff.}$ 2^{19}). How general this custom was among women is indicated in the question which the husband of the Shunamite woman asks: "Wherefore wilt thou go to him to-day? it is neither new moon, nor sabbath" (2 Ki. 4^{23}). The rape of the Shilonite maidens is planned in expectation, and carried into effect in the realization, of the fact of the presence of the daughters of Shiloh at the annual feast of Jahveh (Ju. 21^{6-25}). At the feast that David makes in honor of the removing of the ark of Jahveh, the religious character of which is confirmed by the offering of sacrifices, women are present (2 S. 6^{19}). The legislation of Deuteronomy definitely

[8] As the Philistine religion seems to have been strongly influenced by Semitic religions (cf. Baethgen, *Rel.*, p. 65), it is not altogether irrelevant to call attention to the fact that, little as is known of the Philistine Dagon cult (cf. Baudissin, *PRE*³. *s.v.* Dagon), it is nevertheless evident from Ju. $16^{23\,ff.}$ that men and women alike mingled in the temple precincts and participated in the festive occasions.

provides for woman's presence at the sanctuary at festal seasons (Dt. $12^{12. 18}$ 14^{26} 15^{20} $16^{11. 14}$).[9] In like manner, at that great religious gathering, the reading of the law, in the days of Ezra and Nehemiah, woman appears side by side with man in all the solemnity and joy of the occasion (Neh. $8^{2. 3}$ 12^{43}).

2. *Woman's Participation in the Sacrificial Meals.*

There is full evidence that women were by no means mere idle spectators at these religious gatherings, but that, on the contrary, they shared in every important cultic act. Chief among these were the sacrificial meals. When Elkanah sacrifices he gives to his wives and daughters "portions" (1 S. 1^4).[10] If it were certain that אשׁפר in 2 S. 6^{19} and its parallel 1 Chr. 16^3 means "a good piece of flesh," A.V., or "a portion of flesh," R.V., as some ancient versions render it, and as may well be expected here to complete the triad of such festival occasions, bread, flesh, and wine,[11] it might furnish another instance in earlier times of woman's participation in the sacrificial meal. But the text is altogether too uncertain.[12] But we have by no means need to depend upon uncertain data. The Deuteronomic legislation is as full as it is explicit upon woman's participation in the sacrificial meals and leaves it beyond any question. Regulating what was no doubt an antique custom, it specifies in a number of distinct passages that at the great sacrificial feast at the central sanctuary woman is to have her share (Dt. 12^{12} 14^{22-29} 15^{19-23} $16^{9-12. 13-15}$). An important illustration on a large scale, that this custom existed not simply in law but in actual practice, even in post-exilic times, is furnished by the sacrificial meal at the publication of the law in the time of Ezra and Nehemiah (Neh. 12^{43}).

Additional evidence of a similar character comes to us from a somewhat different source. The Levitical legislation is much concerned with the disposition of that part of the sacrifice which fell to the priest. The material is divided into קדשׁ קדשׁים and קדשׁ.

[9] In view of this definite provision, the regulation "Three times a year shall all thy males appear in the presence of Jahveh" (Ex. 23^{17} 34^{23} Dt. 16^{16}), can not possibly imply the exclusion of woman. But more on that subject below.

[10] The word מנה is a technical term almost exclusively used of the portion of sacrifice that falls to the priest, or of the sacrificial meal that falls to the worshipper (Ex. 29^{26} Lev. 7^{33} 8^{29} 2 Chr. 31^{19} 1 S. 9^{23}). When in later usage the term is widened to cover portions of other meals, the festival character of the meal is still apparent (Neh. $8^{10. 12}$ Esth. 2^9 $9^{19. 22}$).

[11] Cf. Klostermann, *Samuelis*, in loc.

[12] Cf. Driver, *Text of Samuel*, p. 207 f.

The first class may be eaten by the male members of the Aaronic family only; the second class may be eaten by the female members as well (Lev. 10^{12-15} 22^{1-16} Nu. 18^{8-19}). The question, why in the later legislation the women of priestly families were excluded from sharing in the most holy things, need not detain us at this point. The fact that they were permitted to share in the holy things, which was strictly forbidden to outsiders,[13] is in line with the fact of their sharing in the sacrificial meals in general.

Woman's participation in the festal meals has, of course, always been recognized; but its relation to her position in cult has so far not been deemed worthy of notice. The tendency has been to speak of these sacrificial meals, either in a general way, as of a 'family' feast, without recognizing specially, or else ignoring, the female element, or else as of 'feasts' without any particular religious significance (Keil, *Deut.*, 359 f.; Oehler, *O. T. Theology*, Engl. Transl., p. 291; Driver, *Deut.*, p. 143; Benz., *Arch.*, 438; Nowack, *Arch.* ii. 213). Woman's share in them clearly defined, it is yet necessary to call attention to and emphasize the cultic significance of these sacrificial meals.

Eating as an act of worship in connection with sacrifice is a familiar fact in Semitic as well as in other religions. W. R. Smith has made it probable[14] that Semitic religion, as it appears in historical times, is founded on the conception of kinship between the god and the worshipper,[15] and the leading idea in the animal sacrifices of the Semites is that of an act of communion in which the god and his worshipper unite by partaking of the flesh and blood of a sacred victim.[16] This idea finds its fullest expression in the Hebrew ritual. As is known, a distinction is made there between sacrifices which are wholly made over to the god and sacrifices which the god and the worshipper share. To the latter class, with which we are mostly concerned, belonged the זבחים and שלמים, that is, all the ordinary festal sacrifices, vows, and free-will offerings, of which the deity received the blood and the fat of the intestines, while the rest was left to the worshipper for a social feast.

The participation in these sacrificial meals, it is to be noticed, is hedged about with severe restrictions, and invested with the utmost

[13] Cf. Lev. 22. This stands out all the more clearly when the exceptions are taken into account; viz., when the priest's daughter had married a stranger, or was a widow, or divorced and had a child, and so had retired outside of the priestly circle. Cf. Lev. $22^{12f.}$

[14] *Rel. of Sem.*, Lectures vi.–viii.

[15] *Ibid.*, p. 51.

[16] *Ibid.*, p. 209.

solemnity. Levitical legislation emphatically provides that the food must be eaten within a specified time, that is, before there was any danger of putrefaction;[17] otherwise it is to be burned; nothing ceremonially unclean must touch it; the person, ceremonially unclean, who eats of it "shall be cut off" (Lev. 7^{15-21} 19^{5-8} 22^{30}). Similar precautions surround the eating of the priest's portion. That the eating of the priest's portion of every sacrifice constituted a sacrificial meal like that of the worshipper may well be questioned (cf. Benz., *Archäol.*, p. 456 f.), but is of no essential importance in our inquiry. Apart from that, there is every evidence of the sanctity of the food. It is called קדש, it must be eaten in a holy place, the ceremonially unclean are forbidden to eat it, and members of the Aaronic family and household only are allowed to partake of it.

The reason for all these precautions is obvious: sacrifice and the sacrificial meal were acts of communion between the god and the worshipper, and approach to it, or partaking of it, was surrounded by all the possible safeguards that surrounded the approach to the god. Yet woman, as has been shown, had free access to it. It is obvious that the participation in an act of such cultic importance finds a far better explanation in woman's inclusion in the cult than any ignoring or belittling of such inclusion can possibly furnish.

3. *Woman's Participation in the Sacrificial Act.*

In approaching this phase of the question it is necessary to call to mind what is now well recognized, that the act of sacrifice in the Hebrew cult had its own history of development.[18] At first all slaughter was sacrifice; no priest was needed to perform the sacrificial act, the worshipper was in this respect his own priest. Later, with the growth of the ritual and a priestly caste, sacrificing becomes the business of the priest, the worshipper recedes from the altar, and his share in the sacrificial act is confined to the laying of the hand upon the victim,[19] which, if we may judge from the analogy of Lev.

[17] The reason that W. R. Smith assigns for this requirement, viz., that the old sacrificial feasts occupied but a single day, or at most two days, and as the act of eating is part of the service it is to be completed before men break up from the sanctuary (*Rel. of Sem.*, p. 221), does not seem to me to be altogether plausible, and I prefer to follow his view on the same point as expressed in another connection. See p. 203, note 8.

[18] Smith, *Rel. of Sem.*, p. 199 f.; Nowack, *Arch.* ii. 87, 211, 218 f.; Benz., *Arch.*, 405 f.

[19] Lev. 3^2, etc. On the meaning of the custom cf. Smith, *Rel.*, pp. 335 and 401 f.; Benz., p. 453.

16^{21}, was accompanied by a confession of sins. But, whether in its earlier simplicity or in its later limitation, the share of the worshipper in the act of sacrificing cannot but be regarded as an act of the highest cultic significance.

That women brought sacrifices in old Israel and also in later time is so evident that an attempt to prove it seems an act of supererogation. But it is with this point as with many others connected with the whole question: facts otherwise well known have been either forgotten or ignored.

An illustration from old Israel is the sacrifice of Manoah and his wife (Ju. 13^{15-21}), the latter's share in which is expressed in her words לא־לקח מידנו עלה[20] [ומנחה] (vs.^{21}). Of like import perhaps are the words about Hannah (1 S. 2^{19}) בַּעֲלוֹתָהּ[21] אֶת־אִישָׁהּ לזבח את זבח הימים. A valuable testimony to the prevalence of the custom is furnished by the prophet Jeremiah, who speaks of the women of his time as performing the various acts pertaining to sacrifice: they bake cakes, pour out drink offerings, and burn incense (Jer. 7^{18} $44^{15.\ 17\ ff.}$). It is true they do not do this in the service of Jahveh; but it will be observed that they are censured by the prophet, not because they as women overstep their prerogative, but rather because they do it "unto other gods."[22]

For later times we have the clearest testimony to the custom in the Levitical legislation which provides, as is well known, for sacrifices of purification for women (Lev. 12 and 15^{19-23}).

In the absence of definite information on the point, it is not easy to say precisely with what action on the part of the worshipper in bringing a sacrifice according to the Levitical ritual the strictly cultic act began. Oehler, with good reason, as it seems to me, maintains that the sacrificial act began with the presentation of the victim.[23] Benzinger considers it to begin with the laying on of the hand. But in view of the fact that in the sacrifice when the victims are birds the "pressing on of the hand" סמך ידו (Maimonides, בְּכָל־כֹּחַ) was omitted, as Benzinger rightly supposes, and as the priest in that case also did the slaughtering (Lev. 1^{15}), and there would so be left nothing of cultic significance for the offerer, it seems better to regard

[20] Cf. Moore, *Judg.*, in loc.

[21] The construction of the sentence, it seems to me, makes Hannah the subject of לִזְבֹּחַ.

[22] That the emphasis is on this is evident from the terms of 44^{3} and the numerous repetitions of the phrase "unto other gods" ($44^{5.\ 8.\ 15.\ 25}$ 7^{18}).

[23] Oehler, *O. T. Theology*, p. 274.

the presentation itself as a part of the sacrificial act.[24] But whether the presentation itself was a cultic act or not, it is agreed by all that the laying on of the hand was. If there were any need of evidence on this point, it might be furnished by the fact that the Mishna[25] explicitly denies woman the right to perform this act. This is characteristic of the Mishna's treatment of woman's position in the cult, on which more will have to be said in another connection. Here it is sufficient to say that however valuable the Mishna is as a witness to the views of the tradition, it is not a safe guide in the exegesis of any particular passage of Scripture. There is no basis in the text for such a discrimination against woman. The laying on of the hand is the regular feature of the עלה (Lev. 4[24]), and woman's offering is an עלה which, judging from the words תביא and לקחה, she herself was to present אל פתח אהל מועד (Lev. 12[6. 8]). The absence of the specific mention of the laying on of hands cannot be urged against it here any more than it can where the offerer is a man (Lev. 14[19. 20]). From a source of greater value on this particular point than the Mishna it would seem that we have direct testimony that women did touch their sacrifices. In the complaint over the idolatry and sinfulness of the women (Baruch 6[29], the Epistle of Jeremy), the statement occurs: "The menstruous woman and the woman in childbed *touch their sacrifices.*" The reference here is evidently[26] to what is prohibited in Lev. 12[4], and may point to the custom that the women like the men laid hands on the sacrifices which they *offered.* It is possible, however, that the term "touch," as Professor Toy suggests to me, may have reference to the *eating* of the sacrifices by the women of priestly families. But neither the context, which deals with such a variety of cultic acts, nor the term itself, ἅπτομαι (in LXX generally for נגע, הגיע), necessarily requires that meaning. We find, therefore, in ancient Israel and in the time to which the Levitical legislation bears witness that in the act of sacrifice women enjoyed equal rights with men.

4. *Woman's Participation in the Vow, Naziritism, and the Function of the Kedesha.*

The intimate relation which the terms התקדש and the Arabic

[24] The difficulty raised by Köhler (quoted by Professor Day in Oehler's *O. T. Theol.*, p. 275), that the fitness of the animal was not decided until after the presentation, is easily overcome by the simple supposition that such examination preceded the more formal presentation.

[25] *Menachoth* 9[8].

[26] Cf. Zöckler, *Kurgef. Kom.*, on Baruch 6[29].

nadhara (Heb. נזיר, נזר, נדר), sustain to each other, as Wellhausen has pointed out,[27] makes it best to consider them together.[28]

The cultic significance of the vow, Naziritism, and the Kedesha are too well acknowledged by all to require restatement; we simply confine ourselves to woman's relation to them.

I begin with the Nazirite vow as furnishing the fullest and clearest illustration of woman's participation in the cult. The Levitical legislation contained in Nu. 6 aims evidently to regulate a custom that is very ancient (cf. Dillmann, *in loc.*). Now it is a remarkable instance of the truth of my contention that no discrimination is made against woman in her relation to the cult that the whole elaborate ritual with its solemn requirements, its abstinence from all products of the vine, the consecration of the hair, the separation from all defilement, the appearing before the door of the tabernacle with offerings, עלה לחטאת, שלמים, and מנחה, and more especially the hair offering (vs.[18]), all this is introduced with איש או אשה (vs.[2]). The same fact meets us in the regulation of the estimation[29] by which a vowed male or female may be redeemed. The female is there, indeed, valued less than the male, but that this has no bearing on the question of cult is very evident.

In view of this clear evidence of woman's participation in the Nazirite vow, we have reason to suppose that woman is included in

[27] *Heid*, p. 118.

[28] In doing this, and doing it here, I deviate, in the interest of what seems to me correcter method, from Stade, followed by Benzinger and Nowack, who treat of vows under the head of cultic actions, and of Nazirites and Kedesha under the head of holy persons. This is evidently due to a tacit following of the opinion that the Nazirite and the Kedesha were officials. Oehler, who favors such a view (*O. T. Theol.*, p. 295), asserts clearly that Naziritism involved no priestly service, but urges Philo's and Maimonides' inference that there is an intimate relation between the Nazirite vow and the commands of abstinence imposed upon the priesthood. But this similarity appears to me slight ground on which to base the official character of Naziritism. These restrictions are evidently of the nature of taboos incident to a state of consecration, and similar to others, viz., the abstinence from women. (Cf. W. R. Smith, *Rel. Sem.*, p. 462 ff.) They are of too general a character, covering the cases of worshipper and priest alike, to allow such an inference. On the other hand, the evident absence of any priestly service in Naziritism, the tenor of the laws, and the historical illustrations, point to the Nazirite as a devotee rather than an official. The single instance of Samuel, where the Nazirite vow is found in combination with prophetic and priestly functions is counterbalanced by the case of Samson and the Rechabites. The case is somewhat different with the Kedesha. Yet on foreign soil the Kedesha was mainly a devotee, and only in some cases became an official, of which there is no illustration in Hebrew cult.

[29] Lev. $27^{2\,ff.}$.

the legislation of the ordinary vow (Nu. 15^{1-13}), although we find it in a general way addressed to man without specific mention of woman. In fact, this must be the case of the legislation in general, unless we should suppose that the decalogue which is addressed to man has no application to woman. That woman made the ordinary vow is not only seen in the case of Hannah (1 S. 1^{11}), but is taken for granted and regulated in Nu. 30. The restriction this legislation places upon woman's power to vow is of interest in that it affords a glimpse of a contrast between her relations to society and to the cult. If woman is independent, that is, a widow or divorced, her vow is as binding as that of man; if she is still unmarried in her father's house and her father hears her vow without opposing it, or if she be married and her husband hears her vow without opposing it, it is equally binding, but if her father or husband "disallow her in the day that he heareth; none of her vows, or of her bonds wherewith she hath bound her soul, shall stand; and Jahveh shall forgive her, because her father (or husband) disallowed her" (vs.^{6}). The meaning of all this is clear: the *cult* knows here no distinction between man and woman; it is the position of woman in society that introduces the difference.

While it is very evident that the institution of the Kedeshim owes its existence in the Jahveh cult to adoption, its prevalence is well attested.[30] It is not necessary to our purpose to do more at this point than to call attention to the fact that in this lowest and most unnatural form of devotion, as we have found it already in some of the higher, woman appears side by side of man, the קדשות by the side of the קדשים.

5. *Woman's Participation in Prayer.*

If, as Stade does (*Gesch.* i. 487 ff.), we regard prayer equally ancient with sacrifice, usually accompanying the latter, and while permitted and practised elsewhere, properly offered at the sanctuary, it is another important cultic act in which women participated. And I gladly follow Stade in referring to Hannah (1 S. $1^{10 \text{ ff.}}$ 2^{1}) as an example illustrating a number of important points connected with the ancient custom of prayer.

And if again we may follow Stade in associating with prayer as

[30] Cf. Stade, i. 479 f.; Benz., p. 428; Nowack, ii. 132; Driver, *Deut.*, p. 264; Dillmann, *Deut.*, p. 349; W. R. Smith, *Rel. of Sem.*, p. 133; Baudissin, *REP*[3], s.v. *Aschera*, etc.

cultic acts fasting, the blessing, the curse, and the oath,[31] we find woman again participating in them.[32]

6. *Woman's Participation in Consultation of the Oracle and in Theophanies.*

That the oracle and its consultation occupied a very important place in the ancient Hebrew cult is a matter of course.[33] The intimate relation in which the oracle stood to the priesthood speaks for the act of consultation as a cultic rite. That women were accustomed to go to inquire of the oracle is shown by the story of Rebekah (Gen. $25^{22 f.}$), which furnishes us not only with the statement ותלך לדרש את יהוה, but also with the quotation of a very ancient oracular response that could have been addressed to a woman only. Even if Stade's view,[34] that the oracular response represents simply the legend of the origin of the oracle at Beersheba, could be established, which is rather doubtful,[35] the legend itself would remain equally forceful as an evidence of the custom of women's participation in the consultation of the oracle.

In this connection, and as pointing to the same fact, that in the conception of the writers of the period no hindrance existed to the free approach of woman to the divinity, may be mentioned the theophanies to women, of which we have not a few illustrations (cf. Gen. $3^{13 ff.}$ $16^{8 ff.}$ $18^{9 f. 15}$ $21^{17 ff.}$ Ju. $13^{3 ff.}$).

7. *Other Indications.*

There are some other facts in the Old Testament which, while not dealing directly with woman's relation to the cult, yet furnish indirectly an evidence that is very valuable. They are the evidences of a religious consciousness and influence of woman that are difficult to account for on the supposition of woman's exclusion from the cult, and, on the other hand, best accounted for by the fact that she shared in the general religious life.

(1) *The Women's Naming of their Children.* — It seems to have been a somewhat general practice in Old Testament times for women to give the names to their children.[36]

31 Cf. Stade, *Gesch.* i. 489 ff.; Nowack, *Arch.* ii. 259–263, 270 ff.

32 Cf. Jer. 36^{6} Lev. 16^{29} 23^{26-32} Est. 4^{16} Gen. 24^{60} 1 S. 1^{17} 2^{20} Ruth 1^{9}.

33 Cf. Stade, i. 471 ff.; Nowack, ii. 272; Benz., 407 ff.

34 *Gesch.* i. 474, note 2.

35 Cf. Dillmann, *Genesis*, in loco.

36 The following statistics on the point may not be without some interest.

The reason for this custom we need not here discuss. For we are interested at this point not so much in the fact of the naming itself as in the contents of the names given. A number of the names given by the mothers contain a decided religious element: ישמעאל, שמואל, בנואל.[37] But the most striking illustration is the naming of איכבוד (1 S. 4^{21}). A very early tradition represents the wife of Phineas as being crushed by the news of the capture of the ark, and the death of her father-in-law and her husband. And when, in the moment of her death, she gives birth to a son, she names him with her dying breath איכבוד, "Inglorious,"[38] saying גלה כבוד מישראל. Three times in the short passage is the emphasis laid upon the loss of the ark. There is no good reason to doubt this feature of the tradition. But, to say the least, we have here clear evidence that in the thought of the narrator of this early tradition it was quite natural for a woman so to feel the loss of the ark as to hand down to posterity her pain in the very name of her son. Can such deep religious feeling be associated with an exclusion from the cult?

(2) *The Influence ascribed to Hebrew Women in Matters of Religion.*—The Deuteronomic sentiment against women's prose-

Out of 44 cases in which the naming of the children is mentioned in the Old Testament, in 26 it is ascribed to women, in 14 to men, and in 4 to God.

Women name in: Gen. 4^{25} 16^{11} $19^{37.38}$ $29^{32 f. 35}$ (all J) $30^{6.8}$ (E) $^{11.13}$ (J) $^{18.20}$ (E) $^{21.24}$ (J) 35^{18a} (JE) $38^{3.4.5}$ (J) Ju. 13^{24} 1 S. 1^{20} 4^{21} 1 Chr. 4^{9} 7^{16} Is. 7^{14} Ruth 4^{17} (תקראנה).

Men name: Gen. 4^{26} 5^{29} (J) 5^{3} 16^{15} 17^{19} 21^{3} (P) 35^{18b} (JE) $41^{51.52}$ (E) Ex. 2^{22} (J) 2 S. 12^{24} 1 Chr. 7^{23} Job 42^{14} Gen. 25^{25} (יקרא) (J).

God names: Is. 8^{3} Hos. $1^{4.6.9}$.

From the fact that P in the only three cases uniformly ascribes the naming to the father, and does so in the case of Seth (Gen. 5^{3}) in contradiction to J, who ascribes it to the mother (Gen. 4^{25}), it might be supposed that P represents a later custom or tendency. But J and E, and the other early sources, are by no means uniform in ascribing the naming to the mother, as may be seen from the enumeration above. All that can be justly claimed is that in the majority of cases the naming was done by the mother.

[37] Since writing this my attention has been called to Mr. Gray's valuable *Studies in Hebrew Proper Names.* I find my view on the value of the Hebrew names as expressive of religious thoughts, and as throwing "light on the Hebrew religion, and more especially on the popular religion," fully corroborated by him. Cf. p. 10 ff.

[38] It seems to me far better to take the אי as the negative than with Klostermann (*in loc.*) as the exclamation אוי. Cf. Driver, *Text of Samuel*, in loco. Gray, *Studies*, expresses it as his opinion that it is not quite clear what אי, as an element in a proper name, means. Cf. p. 246, note 1.

lytism (spoken of more fully elsewhere) is here in point. While, of course, this proselytism is in behalf of foreign cults, it yet indicates an intense religious interest and influence, scarcely conceivable apart from her share in the cultic life.

Neither may we pass over lightly such expressions as Ruth's וֵאלֹהַיִךְ אֱלֹהָי. It was hardly an empty phrase. If it may be taken, as well it ought to be, and as is so generally done, as an evidence of the early conception of the close union of the god with his land, the personal pronouns are an equally strong indication of woman's share in the religious life.

4. Woman's Relation to the Jahveh Cult as affected by Some Ritualistic Legislation.

1. *The Female in Sacrificial Victims.*

According to the researches of W. R. Smith, a very vital principle underlies the selection of the sacrificial animal, which determines not only the species of the animal but also its sex.[39] It is therefore not without meaning to our inquiry to note whether the sacrificial animal in the Hebrew cult was limited to the male.[40] We should expect that a cult that proscribes woman on account of her sex would also not permit the use of a female victim in sacrifice. But that the latter is not the case in the Hebrew cult is very evident. In earlier practice the female victim predominates (Gen. 15^{9}[E] 1 S. 6^{14} 16^{2}). In the Levitical legislation a discrimination is made in favor of the male in that it is preferred in the more solemn sacrifices, but even there the female victim is by no means excluded. A male is required as a passover-lamb (Ex. 12^{5}), for the עלה (Lev. $1^{3.10}$ 22^{19}); in the חטאת a male is required from an "anointed priest" (Lev. 4^{3}), from the whole people (vs.^{14}), from the ruler (vs.^{23}), while in the case of an ordinary Israelite a female is accepted (vs.$^{28.32}$ and 5^{6}); in the שלמים the victim may be either male or female (Lev. $3^{1.6}$; cf. Mal. 1^{14}). I defer the discussion of the reason for this discrimination; for the present, let it suffice to mention this as simply another fact pointing to the conclusion that the Hebrew cult is not pervaded by any principle that excludes the female sex.

2. *Woman as ceremonially "defiling."*

Both the sexual approach to woman and her condition in childbed or during her courses are regarded in Hebrew custom and legislation,

[39] *Rel. of Sem.*, Lecture viii.

[40] As was the case among the Harranians, quoted by W. R. Smith, p. 280, note 2.

as among many other nations, as ceremonially defiling (1 S. $21^{5f.}$ Ex. 19^{15} Lev. 12 $15^{19ff.}$ Ez. 36^{17} Is. 64^{6} Baruch 6^{29}). The original ground for this legislation lies most probably, as is suggested by Stade,[41] in animism, which regards as unclean and defiling all such persons who are under the influence, that is, possessed by spirits, viz., those that suffer from certain diseases or have done certain acts that stand under the protection of certain spirits. It is, however, perfectly evident that this condition of ceremonial unfitness is only temporary: its removal can be effected. And the very exception of woman's fitness for the cult under those conditions proves the rule of her ordinary inclusion.

3. *Woman not excluded from the Three Yearly Feasts.*

"Three times in the year shall all thy males see[42] the face of the Lord Jahveh" (Ex. 23^{17} 34^{23} Deut. 16^{16}). That this is an old law, and has reference to the three yearly feasts, is evident from the connection in which it is found. But it may well be remembered that its origin, like the origin of all the earliest legislation, was not theoretic but consuetudinary, the result of actual cases presented to the priest for decision. And it may well have had its occasion in the fact that such a law could not be put in effect in the case of woman as easily as in the case of man, and not without contravening the other custom and legislation that excluded her from the approach of holy things at certain periods, just considered. To infer, therefore, from this law woman's exclusion from all cult would be more than it can bear, and is contradicted by all the facts so far adduced. Neither is it a parallel case, as it seems to me, to be cited in connection with the custom that certain holy parts of an ox must not be eaten by women. Smith, *Rel. of Sem.*, p. 281, note 3.

4. *The Law of the Firstlings.*

The law of the firstlings with its emphasis upon the firstborn male might at first sight appear as a very formidable objection to woman's inclusion in cult; but upon careful examination the facts here will be found in harmony with those already adduced.

That the later legislation counts the males only as firstlings cannot be questioned (Nu. $3^{40ff.}$ [P]). But it seems to me altogether doubt-

[41] *Gesch.* i. 483 f.; cf. also Smith's "Notes on Holiness, Uncleanness, and Taboo," in *Rel. of Sem.*, p. 426 ff., and "Taboos and the Intercourse of the Sexes," *ibid.*, p. 435 ff.; Wellhausen, *Heid.*, p. 116.

[42] Not "appear before"; cf. Driver on *Deut.* 16^{16}.

ful whether this was also the case in the earlier legislation. But as this has been assumed, without a dissenting voice, to have always been so, one feels the need of much courage to call it in question. Yet there are weighty considerations against this assumption that have a right to a hearing.

The origin of the consecration of the firstlings is found, as W. R. Smith has pointed out (*Rel. of Sem.*, p. 444), in something of the nature of taboo of the first produce, having its proper parallel in the vegetable kingdom in the law of Lev. $19^{23\,\text{ff.}}$, which ordains that for three years the fruit of a new orchard shall be treated as 'uncircumcised' and not eaten. This being the case, and as we have found no discrimination against female victims in offerings in general, we might argue on general grounds against the probability of an original discrimination here. There is, however, far more direct evidence that no such discrimination existed in earliest times. I mention:

(*a*) The term פֶּטֶר רֶחֶם, or פֶּטֶר שֶׁגֶר. It is repeated so often that we can scarcely go amiss in seeing in it the central idea of the custom and the law. But if this be so, its limitation to a זָכָר practically annuls it by introducing an entirely different element which takes its emphasis. If there be any meaning or force in the פטר, the זכר dissipates it. It does, therefore, seem improbable that they both belonged to the original idea, and far more probable that that was contained in the פטר, irrespective whether it was male or female, in agreement with the idea of the taboo of the first produce. Cf. also the כָּל in כל פטר רחם (Ex. 13^{12} Ez. 20^{26}).

(*b*) W. R. Smith has also called attention to the fact that "in the period immediately before the exile, when sacrifice of firstborn children became common, these grisly offerings were supposed to fall under the law of firstlings (Jer. 7^{31} 19^{5} Ez. 20^{26})."[43] But, this being so, the passage in Jeremiah, stating that that which was done to בניהם was also done to בנתיהם, shows that still at that time the female was included in the law of the firstling.

(*c*) A careful examination of the wording of the texts of the law reveals the fact that the word זכר has only a very doubtful place in them. To facilitate such examination, I present the following tabulated form of the law:

1.— JE. Ex. 13^{2}:

קדש לי כל בכר פטר כל רחם בבני ישראל באדם ובבהמה לי הוא:

[43] *Ibid.*, p. 445.

2.—JE. Ex. $13^{12, 13}$:

והעברת כל פטר רחם ליהוה וכל פטר שגר בהמה אשר יהיה לך [הזכרים] ליהוה:
וכל פטר חמר תפדה בשה ואם לא תפדה וערפתו וכל בכור אדם בבניך תפדה:

3.—E. Ex. 22^{28}: בכור בניך תתן לי:

4.—JE. Ex. $34^{19, 20}$: כל פטר רחם לי וכל מקנך [תזכר] פטר שור ושה:
ופטר חמר תפדה בשה ואם לא תפדה וערפתו כל בכור בניך תפדה:

5.—D. Dt. 15^{19}:
כל הבכור אשר יולד בבקרך ובצאנך [הזכר] תקדיש ליהוה אלהיך:

6.—P. Nu. $3^{40 \text{ ff.}}$: ויאמר יהוה אל משה פקד כל בכור זכר לבני ישראל וגו׳:

It is to be noticed, in the first place, that in passages 3 and 1, evidently the oldest form of the law, no specification is made that the consecrated firstborn must be a male. For I take it that בניך may stand for "thy children" as well as for "thy sons," and, as the term בכר has a feminine as well as a masculine plural, it may be either masculine or feminine. Cf. Ges.-Kautzsch, ed. 26, § 87, 3; and the feminines in והבל הביא גם הוא מבכרות צאנו ומחלבהן וגו׳ in Gen. 4^4.

We note, secondly: If the syntactical position of הזכרים in 2 and the corrupt תזכר in 4 be examined, and compared with the position of זכר in 6, it will be seen that in the first two passages, as well as in 5, the word has all the appearance of not being an original part of the sentence but of being an afterthought, a gloss.

And, thirdly, the term זכר is peculiar to P. JE, it is well known, uses איש ואשתו in the place of P's זכר ונקבה (comp. Gen. $7^{2 \text{ and } 9}$), and the term nowhere else occurs in JE (cf. Brown and Driver's *Gesenius's Lex.*, s.v. זכר).[44] The three facts together, as it seems to me, can lead to but one conclusion, namely, that the term זכר in Ex. 13^{12} 34^{19}, and probably also in Dt. 15^{19}, is due to a later glossing by a source related to P, and that its object was to bring into harmony the earlier with the later custom.

And altogether our examination of the law of the firstlings, far from pointing to an exclusion of the female from cult, is but another indication that in early times no discrimination was made against the female, but that perfect parity existed between the sexes in matters of the cult.

[44] This does not apply to the peculiar form זְכוּר found in Ex. 23^{17} 34^{23}.

5. *Circumcision in its Relation to Woman's Position in Cult.*

The prominence given to the rite of circumcision in the Old Testament will scarcely permit us to pass it without an inquiry as to such a relation. Von Orelli is probably right in his contention that circumcision was practised among the Hebrews in the pre-Mosaic times (cf. *PRE*[3], s.v. "Beschneidung," against Nowack, *Arch.* i. 168). But, as Smend says (*Alttest. Rel.*, p. 37), it was not in ancient Israel a sign of a servant of Jahveh, nor did Moses make it such. Its meaning and application in Arabic heathenism is of service to us here.[45]

The Arabs circumcised the girls also, and made a feast as at a boy's circumcision (Wellh., *ibid.*). Wellhausen's supposition, that the circumcision of girls was not as generally practised as that of boys, seems very likely. But why it may not be regarded in the same light, and why it "hat eher eine natürliche Veranlassung und einen medicinischen Nutzen gehabt," is not apparent. In the absence of definite evidence on this point, the most reasonable supposition is that whatever cultic significance the act had in the case of man it also had in the case of woman. All the evidence we have to form our judgment on the question whether circumcision was practised on girls in early Israel or not is the analogy of the Arabic custom; and the analogy, it seems to me, is stronger than the silence. At any rate, there is no ground to construe that silence into exclusion from the cult. Circumcision, with its religious significance as the sign of Jahveh's covenant with Israel, is a late, exilic view,[46] and is no more a criterion, than the preceding case of the law of the firstborn, for the condition of ancient Israel. And in the same light we must regard all such exclusive prominence given to "males" in the priestly genealogies[47] and laws of temple service.[48]

5. The Hebrew Woman's Relation to the Cult of the Dead and the Worship of Ancestors.

Attention has long since been called to the traces of an extensive cult of the dead in the ancient Hebrew religion, originating most

[45] According to Wellhausen (*Heidenth.*, p. 154 f.; cf. also W. R. Smith, *Rel*, p. 319), the etymology of חתן and its Arabic equivalent points to a connection of circumcision with bridegroom. But perhaps the practice is, like the hair-offering, a representative sacrifice, by which recognition is made of the divine ownership of human life (cf. T. K. Cheyne, *Encycl. Britannica*, s.v. "Circumcision"). In either case we may suppose it to be of cultic significance.

[46] Cf. Smend, *Rel.*, p. 38 f.; Nowack, i. 169 f.

[47] Jos. 17^{2} Ezra $8^{3\,ff.}$ 2 Chr. $31^{16,\,19}$.

[48] Lev. $6^{18.\,29}$ 7^{6} Nu. $3^{15.\,22}$ 1 Macc. $2^{18\,ff.}$, etc.

probably in ancestor worship (Stade, *Gesch.* i. 387 ff.; Nowack, *Arch.* ii. 300 f.; Benzinger, *Arch.*, p. 165 ff.; Smend, *Alttest. Rel.*, p. 112 f.), and finding its analogies in other religions, and particularly in Arabic heathenism (Wellh., *Heidenth.*, pp. 159–164; Goldziher, "Ueber Todtenverehrung im Heidenthum und im Islam," *Muhammedanische Studien* i. 229 ff.).[49]

1. *Woman's Participation in the Various Mourning Rites.*

Apart from such actions as were the natural expressions of grief over the dead, there are certain features in the prevalent mourning customs that had evidently cultic significance, in which women prominently participated.

Jer. 16^{6-8} gives us a pretty complete list of the numerous mourning customs in vogue in Israel. Taking them up in that order we find:

(*a*) The Lamentation. The variety of terms used for the act of lamentation over the dead, אנה, אבל, ספד, נהה, המה, points to its general practice, but the specific technical meaning of קִינָה, with its peculiar rhythm and exclamatory beginning איכה, איך, אי, which has furnished the technical term מְקוֹנְנוֹת (Jer. 9^{16}) for the professional "mourning women,"[50] met with both in ancient and modern Arabia (cf. Goldziher, p. 251; Trumbull, *Studies in Oriental Life*, p. 153 ff.; Stade, *Gesch.* i. 388), and in ancient Babylonia in the female *kalû* (*Records of the Past*, Second Series, ii. 78; Maspero, *Dawn of Civilization*, p. 684), points particularly to woman's principal share in the act.

(*b*) Laceration, הִתְגּוֹדֵד (Dt. 14^1 1 Ki. 18^{28} Jer. 16^6 41^5 47^5 Mic. 4^{14}), finding its parallel in the custom of Arabic heathenism, where the women beat or scratched their faces till the blood flowed.[51]

(*c*) The Hair-offering, קרחה (Am. 8^{10} Mic. 1^{16} Dt. 14^1 and others), especially of women (Is. 3^{24}). See Goldziher, p. 247 ff.; Wellh., *Heid.*, p. 161; Smith, *Rel.*, p. 306 ff.

(*d*) The Sacrifices to or for the dead, and the sacrificial meal connected with it (Jer. $16^{7, 8}$). See Stade, *Gesch.* i. 388 f., 425; Driver, *Deut.*, p. 291 f.; Benz., *Arch.*, 165 ff.; Nowack, *Arch.* i. 196 f.

That these cultic rites were performed *by* men and women alike, and *for* men and women alike, is already clear from the references adduced. It will, however, not be altogether superfluous to empha-

[49] Add W. R. Smith, *Rel. of Sem.*, p. 304 ff.

[50] Cf. also the term השרות קינות (2 Chr. 35^{25}), and יֹדְעֵי נֶהִי (Am. 5^{16}).

[51] Cf. Goldziher, p. 246 f., 253; Wellh., *Heid.*, p. 160; W. R. Smith, *Rel. of Sem.*, p. 304 ff.; Driver, *Deut.*, p. 156; Smith, *Kinship*, 214 ff.

size the force of Jeremiah's words on this point. The calamity of unceremonial burial of which the prophet speaks is one "concerning the *sons* and concerning the *daughters* that are born in this place, and concerning their *mothers* that bare them and concerning their *fathers* that begat them" (vs.^{3}), and for their *fathers* or for their *mothers* (vs.^{7}).

If, while at this point, I may also call attention to the care and interest ascribed by tradition to the patriarchs in the burial of their wives (Gen. 23^{2} 25^{10} $35^{8.\ 19\,f.}$ 48^{7} $49^{31\,f.}$), and to Barzillai's words to David: "Let thy servant, I pray thee, turn back again, that I may die in mine own city, by the grave of my *father* and my *mother*" (2 S. 19^{38}), it will appear how utterly unfounded and erroneous Benzinger's statement is that "ebensowenig wurden der Frau nach dem Tod kultische Ehren zu teil" (*Arch.*, p. 140). It will appear also that the phrases like "to be buried with one's fathers" (1 Ki. 14^{31} 2 Ki. $12^{22\,(21)}$, etc.) may be too narrowly interpreted.

The mourning customs just considered, on account of their being cultic rites, have been taken as the evidences of early ancestor worship among the Hebrews. See the references cited on p. 137. It is not at all of moment to our inquiry to come to a decision on this question one way or the other. But as Stade, followed by Nowack and Benzinger, invariably and specifically asserts woman's exclusion from the cult of the ancestors,[52] I shall endeavor to show that every fact taken by him as pointing to ancestor worship at all points with equal force to woman's inclusion in it. To woman's participation in the various cultic mourning rites, I add now:

2. *The Sanctity of the Tombs of Female Ancestors.*

The grave, as is well known, became in some cases a religious shrine in ancient Israel; that it even became an asylum, and its precincts a *τέμενος* (*ḥima*) as in Arabic heathenism (Goldz., p. 235 f.), we do not know. As this sanctity of the grave is taken as pointing strongly to ancestor worship, it is important to call attention to the fact that prominently by the side of the accounts of the sacred burial places of the patriarchs, of Joseph, of Moses and Aaron, we read of the grave of Rachel with its מצבה (Gen. 35^{20}), of Miriam in Kadesh (Nu. 20^{1}), and of Deborah under the sacred tree near Bethel, the Allon-bacuth being most probably identical with the Deborah-Palm in Ju. 4^{5}. See Dillmann, *Genesis*, in loco, and Moore, *Judges*, in

[52] Stade, *Gesch.* i. 390 f.; Nowack, *Arch.* i. 154, 344, 348; Benz., *Arch.*, p. 140.

loco. In fact, there are more graves of female ancestors mentioned of pre-Mosaic times than of male, including besides those already mentioned those of Sarah, Rebekah, and Leah at Machpelah (Gen. 49^{31}). It is evident, therefore, that whatever religious significance there is in the sanctity of the graves of the ancestors, woman shares in it. This appears also in another fact that may be mentioned here. If we may, with Nowack (i. 177), consider that the ceremony of boring the ear with an awl to the doorpost (Dt. $15^{12\,ff.}$ Ex. $21^{2\,ff.}$), whereby a slave becomes a permanent member of the family, is best explained as a remnant of ancestor worship, the אלהים in these passages referring to the ancestors of the family, we have but another instance of woman's share in the cult, for Dt. 15^{17b} prescribes: "And also unto thy bondwoman shalt thou do likewise."

3. *Woman's Access to and Possession of the Teraphim.*

While it may be true that the evidence that the teraphim were the images of the ancestors of the family, and their consultation a species of manes oracle (Stade, *Gesch.* i. 467; Nowack, ii. 23; Baudissin, *Studien* i. 57), is not altogether full enough to be conclusive, yet it seems to be going too far to the other extreme to say (Moore, *Judges*, p. 380) that there is no evidence. The inference from Gen. $31^{19.\,30\,34}$ 1 S. 19^{13} Ju. 17^{5} that the teraphim were household gods seems to me not much weakened by the reference to Ez. 21^{21}. At any rate, that they were images legitimately used in divination in ancient Israel (1 S. 19^{13} Ho. 3^{4} Zech. 10^{2} Ez. 21^{21}) is generally admitted. It is in this, after all, that the significance of the teraphim in our inquiry lies.

Twice women are mentioned in the Old Testament in connection with the teraphim. Of course, Michal's use of the teraphim (1 S. 19^{13}) contains nothing of cultic significance; all that we may legitimately gather in this direction is that she evidently had free access to the image. But it is entirely different with the case of Rachel (Gen. $31^{19.\,30.\,34}$). Why did Rachel steal the teraphim, the god (it was probably only *one* image, cf. Dillmann, *in loc.*) of her father (אלהי, vs.[30])? We may hardly ascribe it to any other than a religious motive, finding its most plausible explanation in the similar case of the Danites (Ju. 18), whose spies had consulted the oracle of Micah and had received a favorable reply (vs.[5 6]), and then had given the hint to the rest of the tribe to carry it away with them (vs.[14]). The teraphim was employed as an oracle[53]: this explains Rachel's interest

[53] Zech. 10^{2} Ez. 21^{21}.

in it, and so we meet here the Hebrew woman for the first time in our investigation not only as a worshipper but in the possession of the sacred objects employed in oracular inquiry.

This leads us to consider next the intimately related question,

4. *Woman's Relation to the Oracle of the Dead, Necromancy, and the other Cognate Forms of Divination.*

As performing oracular functions (קסם, cf. Wellh., *Heid.*, p. 126 f.; Stade, i. 505; but especially W. R. Smith, *Journal of Philology* xiii. 276 ff.) of the oracle of the dead (described in Is. 8[19] Dt. 18[11] as דרש אל המתים) woman appears officially, as the בעלת אוב, one who has a familiar spirit, in the woman of Endor (1 S. 28). This official character of woman is worthy of special notice. That necromancy was a religious cult is clear from the terms which are used in connection with it. The woman of Endor describes her vision as seeing אלהים (vs.[13]), דרש and קסם are the terms used in speaking of the consultation; the opposition to the cult brands it as a תועבה (Dt. 18[12]) and its approach with the technical terms חִלֵּל (Ez. 13[19]) and טמא (Lev. 19[31]) as ceremonially defiling.[54] The opposition it met with and its frequent mention show how widely and how deeply the cult had entrenched and retained itself in the popular faith. Whether its origin lies in ancestor worship, as Stade supposes, need not be here discussed. This is certain, that we find woman acting in a widespread popular cult in an official capacity, and, judging from the fact that Saul's order is בקשו לי אשת בעלת אוב, occupying the leading position. The latter is confirmed also by the fact that in the often recurring phrase האובות והידענים (Lev. 19[31] 20[6] Is. 8[19] 19[3] etc.) the feminine האובות invariably comes first.[55]

The 'wise woman,' אשה חכמה, and the use made of her (2 S. 14[2] 20[16], also Ju. 5[29] Ex. 35[25]), contains nothing of cultic significance (cf. Smend, *Alttest. Rel.*, p. 91).

But here unquestionably belongs the practice of divination by

[54] For these reasons I cannot follow Driver (*Deut.*, p. 226) when he says that the opposition to the cult was not due to its being considered idolatry but a superstition. It was a rival cult that the opposition fought, and one that was not altogether of foreign origin. Cf. Stade, *Gesch.* i. 425; W. R. Smith, *Jour. of Phil.* xiii. 273 f.

[55] Schwally arrives at the original meaning of זכר, viz. "Todtenbeschwörer," by a combination of it with the Targumic דְכוּרוּ, the translation of the Hebrew אוב, יִדְּעֹנִי, and מְעֹנְנִים (*ZATW.* xi. 179 ff.), but he never mentions the Hebrew בעלת אוב and the numerous references to woman's activity in this religious sphere.

some women mentioned in Ez. $13^{17\,ff.}$. Upon this obscure form of divination the investigations of W. R. Smith (*Jour. of Phil.* xiii. 286 f.) have thrown considerable light. The object of the practice was oracular. According to vs.[22], it was the means of obtaining responses, which according as they were assurances of divine favor or the opposite made man glad or sorry. The means employed were some kind of appurtenances tied to the arm and put on the head. The word כסתות Ephrem Syrus explains as 'amulets,' and ὁ Ἑβραῖος in the Hexapla renders it *φυλακτήρια*. Now, as the Jewish phylacteries were amulets to make prayer more powerful, "we must take it here," says Smith, "that these women invoked the deity — obviously for an omen." Of the nature of the omen the explanation is found in the words: "Ye profane me with my people for (or with) handfuls of barley and crumbled pieces of bread" (vs.[19]). These were the *ἀπαρχαί*, the altar gifts, or, perhaps more likely, the pay for divining, of the same elements as in Syriac divination, and pointing as in that case to "a kind of omen which in its first origin was drawn from the gift of firstfruits at a — Canaanite or Hebrew — sanctuary, with the aid of prayer, such as habitually accompanied rites from which an oracle was sought" (Smith, *ibid.*). If we now associate with this official capacity as the dispenser of the oracle that of the בעלת אוב and Rachel's possession of the teraphim, we have found strong indications, to be corroborated later on, that not only did woman share in the cult as worshipper, but that she also occupied an official position in it.

The term המתנבאות used by Ezekiel to describe this activity of the women suggests naturally a probable connection of it with the most important phenomenon in the question of woman's relation to the cult, namely, the order of the prophetesses.

6. Women as Officials in the Jahveh Cult.

1. *The Prophetesses.*

While the existence and activity of women as prophets in Hebrew religion cannot but be recognized by all, it is of interest to note how variously the fact is treated by moderns. Nowack, in his paragraph on "Seher und Propheten," passes it in silence (*Arch.* ii. 130 f.). Stade (*Gesch.* i. 178) and Montefiore (*Hibb. Lect.* 1892, p. 75) doubt its existence in ancient Israel. The former calls Deborah "eine wirkende weise Frau," and the latter says, "if Deborah was a seer." Professor Moore regards Deborah as a prophetess in the older sense of the word, an inspired woman, and compares her with the German Veleda and Joan of Arc. Smend (*Alttest. Rel.*, p. 90 f.) more readily acknowledges the religious character of the earlier prophetesses. Of Miriam he significantly says that she was probably more prominent than the tradition represents. The only mention of the prophetess in relation to woman's position in religion is made by Benzinger (*Arch.*, p. 140), and he dismisses it with the curt remark that it is the exception that only proves the rule of woman's exclusion from the cult.

But it is a matter of course that no view of woman's relation to the cult can have any weight that leaves out of due consideration such an important fact. And it is no wonder, on the other hand, in view of the isolation with which the phenomenon of the prophetess has been treated, that it should appear as it does to Professor McCurdy (*Hist. Proph. and the Monuments* ii. § 423) as an anomaly (which he mentions only with a word), yielding itself only a little more readily to an explanation (which explanation, however, he does not attempt to give) than her position as judge and queen. It will, therefore, prove no mean confirmation of the correctness of my view of the relation of woman to the cult if it furnishes an explanation, and the only one offered, of this anomaly. That we must in the consideration of this question draw the important modern distinction between the earlier and the later character of prophetesses is very evident. There is exactly the same difference between a Huldah and a Deborah as there is between a Jeremiah and a Samuel.

Of later prophetesses Huldah is the principal example. Noadiah is simply known to us by name (Neh. 6^{14}).

(1) *Huldah* (2 Ki. $22^{14 \mathrm{ff.}}$). — This prophetess comes into the foreground as the chief religious authority at the time of a most intense religious excitement, and in connection with an event that stands without a parallel in its effect upon the development of the religious thought and life of Israel. It is a remarkable fact that the person to whom, at the order of the King of Judah, Hilkiah the priest and Shaphan the scribe, and others equally prominent in state and church, should direct themselves to inquire concerning the meaning of the discovery of the Book of the Law, should be a woman. Equally significant is the nature of the oracular response. For, it must be remembered, it is not a political or moral issue that is up; neither does it concern religion in general. Deuteronomy has chiefly to do with the cult; it is therefore a question of the cult that is brought before the prophetess, and her response is altogether concerned therewith. This interest and authority of the prophetess

Huldah in such a question, being also in perfect accord with the legislation of Deuteronomy itself, which, as has been pointed out above, recognizes woman's share in worship, has a momentous bearing on the question at issue. But important as this testimony is, the full force of it will be best perceived when the office of the prophetess is viewed as it existed in its earlier stages.

(2) *Office of the Earlier Prophetesses.* — There seems to me no sufficient ground to call in question the activity of women as seers in the pre-monarchic period in Israel's history, as has been done by Stade, Montefiore, and others. If early Hebrew tradition is of any historical value whatever, it certainly speaks of a prophetess Deborah as distinctly as of a prophet Samuel, whatever meaning that term may have. In like manner do the earliest traditions prominently associate with Moses and Aaron as head of the Israelitish community their sister, the prophetess Miriam (Mi. 6[4] Ex. 15[20 f.] [E] Nu. 12 20[1] [JE]). But how are we to interpret the term נביאה as used here? There can be but the one way, it seems to me, which has its basis in the explanation in 1 S. 9[9], and according to which the earlier Hebrew נביא was a רֹאֶה or חֹזֶה. To say this in the case of Samuel, and to call Deborah "eine weise Frau," seems an inconsistent choice of terms in order to convey a different meaning of the word when used in speaking of woman. There is not the slightest reason for such a distinction, and, in fact, none is assigned; so it seems but fair to ask that the word be allowed to mean the same thing in both cases, in that of Deborah as in that of Samuel. And all the more so because the principal function of 'judge,' whether in the earlier sense of 'vindicator' or in the later sense of 'giving judicial decisions,' is ascribed to the one as much as to the other (compare Ju. 4[5] and 1 S. 7[16 ff.]; cf. Moore, *Judges*, in loco). If, as may be therefore justly claimed, Deborah was a seer, then all the light which recent investigation has thrown upon the origin and function of the seer is at our service. If the office of seer, as is held by Stade (*Gesch.* i. 468–473), had its origin in the belief that some persons were specially possessed by the divinity; if its function was, by means of visions, to reveal the divine will; if, as is illustrated by the case of Samuel, it was intimately connected with the sanctuary; if, as is indicated by the relation of the Hebrew and Arabic terms, כהן, *kâhin*, the offices of priest and seer were once identical, and the old Israelitish priesthood originated in the settlement of some seers at a permanent sanctuary (cf. Wellh., *Heid.*, p. 130 ff., 167), then the function of the prophetess had an origin in common with the highest cultic function in Israel, the priest-

hood, and this function was, at one time, open to some extent to women. To claim this for Samuel seems perfectly natural, for, of course, we find in his case clear indications of such a fusion of seer and priest. But the inference that such was the case also when woman filled the same office is perfectly reasonable, and by no means lacks more definite confirmation. Woman's relation to the teraphim, the oracle of the dead, and divination, as developed above, is here in point, but additional evidence in the same direction and within the Jahveh cult comes to us in the case of Miriam.

(3) *Miriam.* — In Nu. 12 (referred to also in Dt. 24^{9}), belonging to the earliest tradition (JE), we have a detailed account of an incident which purports to involve the question of the relative official rank of Moses, Aaron, and Miriam. The contention was occasioned by the marriage of Moses with a Cushite woman, and partakes of the nature of a family quarrel. "Hath Jahveh indeed spoken only with Moses? hath he not spoken also with us?" (vs.[2]), say Miriam and Aaron; and as Dillmann has pointed out (*in loc.*), the feminine ותדבר would show that Miriam was the instigator. The claim that her words imply is prophetic rank and authority for herself and Aaron equal to those of Moses. In the settlement of the dispute by the intervention of Jahveh, it becomes apparent that her claim of prophetic rank is not denied, and she, as well as Aaron, bears the title of 'prophet'; only to Moses is ascribed the official preëminence, while she, as the instigator of the insubordination, has to bear the brunt of the punishment. While the incident thus brings out Moses' preëminence, it at the same time asserts the official equality of Miriam with Aaron. That the whole incident is brought into intimate connection with the אֹהֶל מוֹעֵד, the centre of the religious cult, is certainly significant. If to this be added the facts, that occasion is taken to state that Miriam is the sister of Aaron (Ex. 15^{20}), and that in the earlier genealogical list her descent is traced back to Levi (Nu. 26^{59} 1 Chr. 6^{3}; Ex. 6^{20} [P] does not mention her), while throughout she is conspicuously associated with Aaron and Moses as a leader of the religious community, the conclusion can scarcely be avoided that, as Deborah like Samuel, so Miriam like Moses and Aaron, is an example of a seer in whom, in the manner of that time, the functions of prophet and priest are combined. The probability of this inference is heightened, if in this connection again we call to mind the activity of prophetesses in other Semitic religions, and woman's part as diviner in connection with the oracles later proscribed by the religion of Jahveh.

2. *Women as Officials in the Tabernacle and the Temple.*

I must now call attention to the direct testimony on woman's official position in the Jahveh cult as contained in the repeated mention of woman's service in the tabernacle.

The passages are הַצֹּבְאֹת אֲשֶׁר צָבְאוּ פֶּתַח אֹהֶל מוֹעֵד (Ex. 38[8]) and הַנָּשִׁים הַצֹּבְאוֹת פֶּתַח אֹהֶל מוֹעֵד (1 S. 2[22b]). The text in Samuel beginning with ואת אשר is almost unanimously regarded as an interpolation. (See Driver, *Text of Sam.*, p. 26; Kittel in Kautzsch's *Heilige Schrift d. A. T.;* Klostermann's *Samuel;* Budde's *Samuel.*) The evidence that the context speaks of a הֵיכָל and not of an אֹהֶל, and that the passage in question ascribes to the sons of Eli a sin entirely different from that of vs.[12 ff.] (see Stade, *Gesch.* i. 199, note 2), is far stronger than the absence of the passage from the LXX in Codex Vaticanus, which is, moreover, somewhat counterbalanced by its presence in Codex Alexandrinus and in Lucian's recension. The fact of the insertion of the passage in Samuel seems best explained as originating in a marginal note suggested by Ex. 38[8].

There is no such question of text connected with the reference in Exodus; it belongs to P, and is definite and clear enough for our purpose.

We must first determine, as far as possible, the meaning of the word צבא as used here. The versions exhibit a marked variation in translating the word. The LXX has for הצבאת אשר צבאו in Ex. 38[8] τῶν νηστευσασῶν αἳ ἐνήστευσαν; Cod. Alex. translates הנשים הצבאת in 1 S. 2[22b] by τὰς γυναῖκας τὰς παρεστώσας (Swete, *in loc.*). The Vulgate translates in Ex. *quae excubabant* and in S. *quae observabant;* in Targ. and Pesh. it is paraphrased 'who prayed' and 'who came to pray' (see Driver, *in loc.*). But there can be no question that צבא has in the Priest's Code the very decided technical signification of 'to render service in connection with the tabernacle in a Levitical capacity' (cf. Nu. 4[23. 30. 35. 39. 43. 47] 8[24. 25]); by its side is usually found the synonym עֲבֹדָה, and the LXX translates it by λειτουργεῖν and λειτουργία. The attempts, therefore, of the ancient versions, as also the A.V.'s 'assemble' (the R.V. correctly renders in Ex. 38[8] "the serving women which served at the door of the tent of meeting," and refers in the margin to Nu. 4[23] and 8[24]), must be regarded as inadmissible, and evidently due to a hesitancy to allow the word to mean the same thing when used in reference to women as when used in reference to men. And such attempts are not any more admissible when the term is limited to express the performance of "menial duties" by the women (Driver); or when there is simply added to these the duties of performing the sacred dances and choral songs (Dillmann, Strack). The fact is, we do not know in what particular the service of the women consisted, but we do know that, whatever the nature of the service, it is described by the same term used for the Levitical service rendered in connection with the tabernacle.

The remark of Nowack (*Arch.* ii. 69, note) that we do not hear in the older accounts of women who serve in the sanctuary, suggests the inquiry whence the information contained in Ex. 38[8] and perpetuated in 1 S. 2[22b] originated. To regard it as haggadic, late Jewish fiction (Popper; Wellhausen, *Composition des Hexateuchs* u.s.w., 1889, p. 147) is out of the question. There is in late Jewish history no indication of a tendency to place women in positions of the cult; both the low estimation in which woman is held and the high estimation with which increasingly the ritual is regarded are against such an idea; the tendency is all the other way. It seems to me that the reference to the service of woman in the passage in Exodus is to something antiquated, something that had long passed even in the time in connection with which it is mentioned. It seems a futile effort to contend, like Dillmann and Keil, over the notion of time the participle צֹּבְאֹת conveys: Keil claiming that it does not imply that they had served there before the erection of the sanctuary, but only from that time forward they did perform service there; and Dillmann, that it does not mean that they served later, but that they served until now. It is the צָבְאוּ that will more readily render service here, yielding itself easily to the tense of the pluperfect; the passage can be rendered: "And he made the laver of bronze, and the base thereof of bronze, of the mirrors of the serving women which *had served* at the door of the tent of meeting." In accordance with this, it is not to be supposed that the צבאת contributed their hand-mirrors as a תְּרוּמָה (Dillm.), but on the analogy of Nu. 17[2-5] (Eng. Ver. 16[36-40]), where the censers left by the Korahites, because of their sanctity through former use, are beaten out into plates for a covering of the altar, and are so turned into another sacred use, so here, the mirrors left behind by the women are put to another sacred service. It is very probable that in both cases we have to do with reminiscenses, embodying Levitical traditions, attached to the sacred utensils of the sanctuary, which were in some cases termed זִכָּרוֹן (Nu. 17[5]). And, although this notice is found in P and is probably a later addition even there, that does not preclude its being based upon very ancient tradition. The אהל מועד

in the Priest's Code is an elaborate affair and not historical, but E knows of an אהל מועד, tells us of its erection, and gives its name (Ex. 33^{7-11}), and also, as has been shown above, brings Miriam in close connection with it. In view of these facts, it is safe to say that the passages in Exodus and Samuel, though late themselves, are in perfect harmony with, and probably embody, an ancient tradition according to which, in early times, women held some official position in the sanctuary of Jahveh.

A side light upon woman's official position in the Jahveh cult comes to us also from the references in the Old Testament to the women singers. There are four distinct classes of these, one of which, the שָׁרוֹת, mentioned in passages like 2 S. 19^{35} Jer. 31^{4} Ec. 2^{8} and Is. 23^{16}, sang evidently only for social amusement, and may here be passed by with the mere mention. The other three classes will find the simplest explanation when considered in their relation to the religious cult.

(1) *The* מְקוֹנְנוֹת *who chant the* קִינוֹת. — Their official relation to, and prominence in, the cult of the dead have been considered above. See p. 137.

(2) The מְבַשֶּׂרֶת, εὐαγγελιζομένη, is mentioned by that name only in Ps. $68^{12\,(11)}$, and the term is also applied to Jerusalem in Is. 40^{9}; but the function of the מבשרת, to announce and celebrate a victory by vocal and instrumental music and dances, finds frequent mention in the Old Testament (Ex. 15^{20} Ju. 5^{1} 11^{34} 1 S. 18^{6} Ps. $68^{26\,(25)}$; cf. also 2 S. 1^{20}). That these choral dances were at least of a semi-religious character will scarcely admit of doubt. These were the "wars of Jahveh," and He Himself is יהוה צבאות: the celebration of victory[56] must have partaken of a religious character. This becomes all the more evident from the religious element contained in some of these songs preserved to us (see Ex. 15^{21} Ju. $5^{3\,ff.}$ Ps. 68 Judith $15^{12\,ff.}$ $16^{1\,f.}$). These facts have naturally enough led some to suppose that the particular service that the women according to Ex. 38^{8} and 1 S. 2^{22} rendered was the sacred choral dances. It is very probable that the term צבא may cover, but there is no reason to suppose that it exhausts, this part of woman's service.

(3) *Women Singers in the Temple Choir.* — Neh. 7^{67} and the parallel passage in Ezra 2^{65} furnish a more direct reference to woman's participation in public religious song. In Neh. 7^{67}, a register which has every appearance of having been drawn up under Zerubbabel

[56] "The Hebrew phrase for opening war is 'to consecrate war' (קדש מלחמה), and warriors are consecrated persons." — W. R. Smith, *Rel. of Sem.*, p. 383.

and incorporated by Nehemiah in his Memoir (cf. Driver, *Introd.*, p. 513, and Stade, *Gesch.* ii. 98), the statement occurs that among the returning exiles were found "245 singing men and singing women." (In the parallel passage in Ezra, probably derived immediately from Neh., the number given is 200.) There is not the slightest reason to suspect the text, and Oettli's suggestion (*Kurzgef. Komm., Die geschichtlichen Hagiographen*, Ezra, in loco) that the context would lead us to expect 'animals' viz. שורים which, by a misunderstanding, was corrupted into משררים and to which was then added the feminine, is entirely uncalled for and too clumsy. Neither is it a happy suggestion that the function of these singers was secular. Is it likely that this company of religious enthusiasts, returning to a desolate home, had carried with them this number of singers for secular amusement? Rashi supposes that they furnished the music during the glad procession in the return from the exile. If this be not more ideal than real, their service would scarcely have ceased with their arrival at Jerusalem.

This reference to women singers, it seems to me, finds its simplest explanation in the supposition that not only did women in early Hebrew history participate in religious song, but that they furnished such sacred music as was used in sacred worship, and that, even in this later time, women still held positions in the temple choirs. There is some Jewish tradition to this effect. Schechter (*Studies in Judaism*, p. 316) makes the statement that "if we were to trust a certain passage in the 'Chapters of R. Eliezer,' we might perhaps conclude that during the first temple the wives of the Levites formed a part of the choir." (Unfortunately Schechter's reference is too indefinite for verification.) It is therefore altogether probable that when we read of music at the religious festive occasions, e.g. the dedication of the walls of Jerusalem (Neh. $12^{27\,ff.}$), it will best harmonize with the statement concerning those 'singing women' to suppose that they contributed their share of music as members of the singer's guild, the בְּנֵי הַמְשֹׁרְרִים of that time. We have here, therefore, an additional indication of women's official position in the Jahveh cult.

www.ingramcontent.com/pod-product-compliance
Lightning Source LLC
Chambersburg PA
CBHW021445090426
42739CB00009B/1657
9783337315993